The Quick Guide to

Agile Project Management for Learning

Megan Torrance
TorranceLearning
© 2017
Iteration 3.0
ISBN: 978-1977977977

Welcome to your Agile journey. This book will get you started.
A workshop or class will give it some context. Learn more online:
www.torrancelearning.com/llama

How it all got started

I began my career in a highly structured project management
culture. Marvelously nested flow charts and corresponding Gantt
charts mapped out each step and each sub-step and the resources
needed for each type of project. With all this pre-planning to
get a project ready to start, I couldn't help but feel I was failing
miserably when, about 2 weeks into the project, something had
changed and I needed to re-plan everything. Regardless of the
amount of pre-planning, the end of each project phase involved a
lot of late nights and a fair amount of panic.

In our early days at TorranceLearning, I threw out the structured
project planning methods. We were doing much more creative
learning projects so Gantt charts clearly weren't going to work!
We gave ourselves lots of time for the creative instructional design
process to happen. Without a plan, we had no idea if we were on
track or not until very close to a design deadline. We still had a lot
of late nights and a fair amount of panic.

Our production process at that time was a stark contrast: we
knew the steps to take, we could estimate each step and we had
easy benchmarks to know if we were on schedule or not. So we
had something going right. My software development friends
introduced me to Agile. It took me a few years to get our Agile
processes to where we needed them to be for learning design and
development projects, and we're still adjusting and improving the
approach.

As I looked at our approach, I realized that it's a lot like traditional
Agile, with a few important tweaks. Hence, LLAMA: the Lot Like
Agile Management Approach.

Gratitudes

This journey, of which this book is a key part, has truly been an effort of Generous Collaboration, one of TorranceLearning's core values.

Iterations 1 & 2

Deep appreciations go to: Helene, Dianne and Rich for their Agile inspiration; Marisa, Catherine, Dianne, Kathy and Phil for the nudge to just "Write the d%$# book"; John, Frank and Peggy for believing in the journey; Michelle and Frank (again!) for inspired and patient design and editing; our clients for entrusting us with the care of their learners; and the entire TorranceLearning team who live it together every day, helping people be more competent and confident in their work.

Iteration 3

I want to express my gratitude to the thousands of people who have bought a book, attended a conference session or participated in a LLAMA workshop. The success of this approach and its resonance with so many is truly uplifting. These encounters improve LLAMA continuously.

And to the TorranceLearning team, a cadre of talented individuals who inspire and challenge me every day.

How to use this book

You'll find in short order that this book isn't a how-to book. Rather, it's a guide for your project management. Some of it applies to whatever project approach you're using. Some of it is Agile-specific. Some of it will enhance your instructional design as well as your project management. I hope you'll find it as a resource when you need to:

Get inspired

Get out of trouble

Use LLAMA for the first time

Share LLAMA with others

Start up a project

Assess project status

Debrief a project

Teach your team

Teach your clients

Take notes and reflect on an idea

Attend a LLAMA workshop

SECTION 1

BUILD THE BUSINESS CASE

Articulate why current approaches to project planning are lacking to convince decision makers (including your own team).

1

Practice > Principle

When you take an agile approach to Agile, you're able to make the process work for you, instead of you working for the process.

Take what you need from this book and apply it to your own work context.

2

"Do more of what works, and
do less of what doesn't."

Kent Beck, author of
Extreme Programming (XP) Explained

3

Projects need to keep up with an ever-increasing rate of change.

In fact, if a project doesn't change during the design and build process, it may not be that interesting or useful.

4

The first day of a project is
the worst day to plan what
the end product will be
(and how much it will cost).

5

It's folly to assume that the project sponsor knows everything they want at the beginning of the project.

Any set of meaningful requirements is subject to change. Locking stakeholders into a set of requirements defined before they really understand what they want is incredibly risky.

6

Agile is a joyful way to work.

Nothing feels so good as to actually accomplish something toward a goal every day.

7

Instructional design and development are not linear assembly line processes, and should not be managed as such.

8

If we do not come up with a brilliant idea that might change things mid-project, we're not fully engaged creatively.

This doesn't mean that EVERY new idea is pursued.

9

Agile works best with teams, and on projects.

Projects are temporary, unique and creative, and therefore need an empirical control process such as Agile.

10

Every day you learn something new about the project you're working on.

11

"The need to predict the future is great. Our ability to do so is minimal."

Richard Sheridan, Menlo Innovations

12

ADDIE and other waterfall methods are reasonable.

Waterfall methods work when it is possible to know everything at the start of a project.

13

ADDIE approaches a perfect world in a highly linear fashion.

It attempts to reduce risk by doing all the analysis up front.

14

Isn't everything "agile"?

At least three distinct uses of the word "agile" are in use in the training industry.

Content Agility is the capability to deliver learning material in a variety of formats. It is a "write once, publish many" approach.

Learning Agility is Korn/Ferry's term for a person's capability to handle new problems and opportunities based on prior learning and experience.

Agile Project Management is a method for managing creative or empirical project processes, one in which team members experiment and observe to improve the product as it is developed.

SECTION 2

DESCRIBE AGILE

Explain Agile's basic principles to someone else.

15

Agile is an iterative, incremental method of guiding design & build projects in a highly flexible & interactive manner, focusing on maximizing customer value and fostering high team engagement.

16

LLAMA is an iterative, incremental method of guiding instructional design & build projects in a highly flexible & interactive manner, focusing on maximizing customer value and fostering high team engagement.

17

THE AGILE MANIFESTO

We are uncovering better ways of developing software by doing it and helping others do it.

Through this work we have come to value:

Individuals and interactions over processes and tools.
Working software over comprehensive documentation.
Customer collaboration over contract negotiation.
Responding to change over following a plan.

That is, while there is value in the items on the right, we value the items on the left more.

www.agilemanifesto.org

18

THE AGILE PRINCIPLES

Our highest priority is to satisfy the customer through early and continuous delivery of valuable software.

19

THE AGILE PRINCIPLES

Deliver working software frequently, from a couple of weeks to a couple of months, with a preference to the shorter timescale.

20

THE AGILE PRINCIPLES

Business people and developers must work together daily throughout the project.

21

THE AGILE PRINCIPLES

Build projects around motivated individuals. Give them the
environment and support they need, and trust them to get
the job done.

22

THE AGILE PRINCIPLES

The most efficient and effective method of conveying information to and within a development team is face-to-face conversation.

23

THE AGILE PRINCIPLES

Working software is the primary measure of progress.

24

THE AGILE PRINCIPLES

Agile processes promote sustainable development. The sponsors, developers and users should be able to maintain a constant pace indefinitely.

25

THE AGILE PRINCIPLES

Continuous attention to technical excellence and good design enhances agility.

26

THE AGILE PRINCIPLES

Simplicity — the art of maximizing the amount of work not done — is essential.

27

THE AGILE PRINCIPLES

The best architectures, requirements and designs emerge from self-organizing teams.

28

THE AGILE PRINCIPLES

At regular intervals, the team reflects on how to become more effective, then tunes and adjusts its behavior accordingly.

29

Agile is as much an attitude as it is a project management method.

30

ADDIE and Agile are not necessarily incompatible.

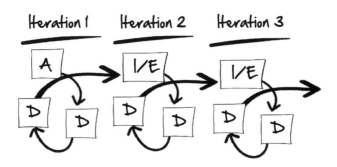

SECTION 3

DEFINE THE GOAL

Begin a project with a shared vision
of success and scope.

31

Your goal is not to create training.

It's to:

Increase Revenue

Decrease Cost

Improve Service or Product

Grow People's Capacity

Comply with Rules & Regulations

Serve the Mission

32

Likewise, the learner's goal is not to complete training.

SECTION 4

WRITE LEARNER PERSONAS

Use learner personas as a guide
to instructional design.

33

A learner persona is an archetypal learner.

Learner personas provide insights for the team and a constant reminder of the reason for building the training. They're incredibly useful members of your team.

34

There is only one primary learner.

The primary learner persona helps you make better design decisions.

35

How do you choose only one primary persona?

- Quantity
- Business Risk
- Impact
- Opportunity
- Turnover
- Degree of Difficulty
- Etc.

SECTION 5

DEFINE SCOPE WITH STORIES

Write learner stories to define scope
and plan the project.

36

Stories capture business needs and performance outcomes in a format that's useful for planning and production.

Stories define scope. They are meaningful to sponsors and users. When we use Cathy Moore's Action Mapping to define stories, we then tie them to actual performance outcomes of the project.

37

Stories are the core of the scope definition and project planning process.

We ...

1. Write Stories
2. Estimate Stories
3. Prioritize Stories
4. Assign Stories
5. Build Stories
6. Track Stories
7. Evaluate Stories

Agile Explained, Menlo Innovations

38

Traditional Agile Story:
As a _____ I want _____
so I can _____ .

This covers the WHO, WHAT and WHY aspects of each piece of desired functionality.

39

Stories are INVEST-U

Each story card should meet the INVEST-U criteria:

I ndependent

N egotiable

V aluable

E stimatable

S mall

T estable

U nderstandable

40

Use story mapping for
building performance support
and tools like software.

41

Use Cathy Moore's Action Mapping to define stories for learning projects.

42

Anyone can write a story at any time.

Typically, the first set of stories are written by the Instructional Designer, stakeholder, sponsor, and SME in the beginning of the project. Stories can be written and added by anyone throughout any stage of the project. It is the responsibility of the Project Manager to hold the stories and keep track of them. The Project Sponsor prioritizes the stories for work.

43

The only stories you work on are ones that have been authorized by the sponsor.

44

There are no bad ideas,
just some that won't ever
get implemented.

Stories are regularly reprioritized.

45

Prioritize stories based on value to the learners.

46

Sometimes your stories
sprout stories.

Large related groups of stories are called "epics."

47

There are often many tasks
associated with a story.
With LLAMA we work on
tasks that support stories.

Break stories down into smaller stories and tasks until they
are a meaningful size. What's meaningful? It's meaningful if you
can reasonably define and estimate the work effort. Note that
Agile software teams usually plan by stories, not by tasks.

SECTION 6

ESTIMATE THE WORK

Estimate the work effort required
to complete the stories.

48

Estimate fearlessly based on what you think it will take to do the work, with no padding.

49

Estimate in increments of
1.2.4.8.16.32.64 or
1.2.3.5.8.13.21.34

50

If the estimate is between
2 estimating values,
use the larger one.

51

If you're estimating in more than 8 hour increments, break down the task into smaller pieces of work.

52

The person who does the work estimates the work.

Exceptions:

- an experienced person needs to guide the process.
- the project sponsor puts boundaries on the value of the story, and therefore its scope.

53

Estimate the work *effort*
(hours spent on task),
not the *duration*
(when you'll be finished).

54

An estimate is just that.
An estimate.

55

Why might an estimate be wrong?

You're over-doing it. Or under-doing it.

You don't have the right skills to do it.

The story is not well-defined.

The story is misunderstood.

You're putting more (or less) effort into the story than it's worth.

Because it was just an estimate.

56

When the estimate is wrong ...

1. Speak up as soon as you know something's awry.

2. Say "thank you."

3. Understand why.

4. Figure out what to do next.

5. Communicate with the client.

SECTION 7

PLAN THE WORK

Prioritize and schedule work.

57

Define at the outset what type of project this is.

It's just one of the three:

Fixed budget

Fixed time

Fixed scope

58

Scope is rarely ever frozen.

Think of scope in terms of both depth and breadth of coverage.

59

Break large projects down into smaller ones by phase, by module, by learner type, by medium ...

... anything you can do to get a better handle on things.

60

The Project Sponsor sets the priorities.

The Project Manager keeps track of priorities as well as the unprioritized stories. When in doubt, do not second guess the sponsor's priorities. Ask.

61

High priority stories are recognizable.

They are the ones that contain more urgent business needs.

They are the ones for which we have more consensus around their value.

They already have more detailed specifications.

More decisions have already been made about them or are easily made.

They are typically easier to estimate (because of the above).

62

Zero-Surprises
Project Management

1. Break big things in to little ones.

2. Plan from the big to the little.

3. Work from the little to the big.

If 2 & 3 don't match, start talking.

4. Make it visual.

63

At no point should the project's status be a mystery.

Status is updated on each task or story as it's worked.

64

Define your duration.

Some like to have 2-week iterations. Some use 30 days or a month. Smaller projects call for shorter iterations. For a 2-day project, iterate every 2-4 hours.

Strict Scrum practice calls for a defined and regular sprint length and the team works to accomplish as much as possible in that timeframe.

A LLAMA iteration is typically as long as it needs to be to reach the next deliverable review, typically 2-3 weeks.

65

As long as a product exists,
there is a backlog.

Backlog is the set of stories you have not yet delivered.

66

Make a story or task card
for the unexpected ...
because you know it's coming.

SECTION 8

LATHER, RINSE, REPEAT

Plan for small, meaningful iterations
that allow for review and adjustments
of the work.

67

"Make small
mistakes faster.
Skip the big mistakes."

Agile Explained, Menlo Innovations

68

Think about it like building a bus.
Version 1

You're assigned to build a bus. You start off by building the engine, then optimizing it like crazy. Two weeks later, the project sponsor arrives in your shop.

"Can we take it for a test drive?"

You start listing the engine's technical specifications. You describe your victory in finding just the right

components. You show off the chrome fashion styling and the embossed logo.

"That's nice. Can we take it for a drive?"

No, but we have these really nice little pink rhinestones over here. Aren't they great?

You're only two weeks into the project. Why would you want to test drive?

69

Think about it like building a bus.
Version 2

You're assigned to build a bus. You start off by building a rough skeleton of the bus, with a basic frame, a basic engine, a steering wheel and something to sit on. Two weeks later, the project sponsor arrives in your shop.

"Can we take it for a test drive?"

Sure! Let's go.

"This is nice. But I forgot to tell you that we are going to be driving this bus in Ireland so the steering wheel needs to be on the other side."

Sure thing!

You're only two weeks into the project. Why can the requirements change like this?

70

Think about it like building a bus.
Version 3

You're assigned to build a bus. You start off by building a rough skeleton of the bus, with a basic frame, a basic engine, a steering wheel and something to sit on. Two weeks later, the project sponsor arrives in your shop.

"Can we take it for a test drive?"

Sure! Let's go.

"This is nice. But you know what would be really cool? What if we could make it amphibious, too?!?!

"Can you do that?"

Sure thing!

You're only two weeks into the project. Why can you accept radical changes to the plan?

71

The MVP is your BFF.

The MVP is the Minimum Viable Product, the most basic version of the project at each iteration. It means you're getting something truly viable out into the real world to get feedback on it, before you get too many bells and whistles on it. It will become your Best Friend Forever.

72

Your job is to organize stories so you can address them in chunks and start planning phases of work.

Try these:

By learner

By time during the work process

By level of skill

By medium or delivery platform

By priority / release schedule

By language

By SME availability

73

"Do the simplest thing that
can possibly work."

Kent Beck, author of
Extreme Programming (XP) Explained

74

Iterations are like eating a cake in slices, not layers.

You get to see how all the parts will work together, instead of one at a time. Mmm. Delicious.

75

Why Iterate?

- You always have something usable.

- You catch errors early.

- You don't get too far off track.

- It's easier to estimate because the pieces are smaller.

- It's psychologically more satisfying.

76

"Form follows failure."

You learn from your mistakes, refine the design as you get feedback and make adjustments accordingly. Release often. Listen well.

Agile Explained, Menlo Innovations

77

With Agile you'll *expect* and *accept* change.

With each iteration, you'll try to find as many changes as you can. The client project sponsor then works with you to determine which ones get worked on in the next iteration.

78

The project sponsor defines what "done" looks like.

Early in the project you'll define with the project sponsor what consitutes a completed project. With each iteration review, you'll want to review that definition of "done." Keep iterating until the project runs out of time, budget or meaningful things left to change, all of which are defined by the project sponsor.

79

Megan's Rules for Iterating

1. It does real work.
2. Someone (like the learner) has to use it.
3. You gather data.
4. You use that data to inform the next iteration.

SECTION 9

AGILE PRACTICES IN ACTION

Use best practices to make your
implementation more effective.

80

Requirements are constantly changing. Use the rituals of Agile to bring stability for the team.

It's been referred to as the "ceremony" of Agile. Weekly meetings, daily sync-ups, and regular iterations all provide structure and ritual to otherwise constantly shifting work.

81

Sometimes you'll join an Agile (often Scrum) team.
Part 1

The #1 complaint of these trainers is that there's no stable documentation upon which to build training. That means that the Agile team is doing something right.

82

Sometimes you'll join an Agile (often Scrum) team.
Part 2

... and you can typically expect:

- few tasks at the beginning of the project.
- more tasks in sprints that are tied to releases (compare with sprints for iterations that will not be released to end users).
- more tasks toward the "end" of the project.
- a general lack of stable documentation upon which to base your training.

83

Sometimes you'll join an Agile (often Scrum) team.
Part 3

... and you'll be incredibly frustrated with the process unless:

- you are prepared for constant change.
- you accept that the underlying product could (should?) change with each iteration.
- you ensure that training becomes part of the user stories.

84

Backlog is better than inventory.

Backlog is approved work not yet done. Inventory is work that's done but not yet delivered. Inventory is wasteful. If you "build ahead" you might find that the need has changed before you have the chance to deliver. You might make different decisions, find out what you've done just isn't necessary, the budget gets cut for that part of things, etc.

85

Hold a daily meeting to touch base with everyone on the team.

It's called a Scrum meeting, huddle, stand-up, sync-up, or whatever you want to call it.

86

Get retrospective!

At each iteration, milestone or surprise event, take time to review & tune the team's process.

Ask what was enjoyable? Frustrating? Puzzling?

What should we do more of? Do less of? Keep doing?

87

When the terrain differs from the map, the terrain wins.

88

Educate new team members on how you work with Agile.

89

Educate your project sponsors
on how you work with Agile.

90

Educate your vendors
and partners on how you
work with Agile.

91

Agile creates a WDWT (work-directed-work-team) environment. Be ready for it.

With Agile, it's very clear what each person should do next and there's a lot less wondering about what everyone is working on.

Agile creates a culture built on transparency and accountability.

92

Project planning becomes everyone's job.

93

People-pleasers,
brown-nosers and
over-achievers
struggle with Agile.

94

Don't be a scope creep.

Keep a tight rein on scope by sticking to the stories and working only on the ones that have been authorized, in the way in which they've been authorized.

95

Celebrate success
frequently in large
and small ways.

96

Lighten up.

Nothing here is an absolute. It's not dogma. Use what works for you if the core premise of an adaptable project management method is applicable for you.

SECTION 10

CREATE THE ENVIRONMENT

Use creative space and team practices
to make LLAMA more effective.

97

Get old school to get started with Agile.

Use 3x5 cards, sticky notes, cork boards and markers. It's easier to keep everything front and center when it's physical.

Added bonus: you can explain what you're doing each time someone stops by your wall and asks what all that stuff is.

98

Open room
+ visual communication
= the room communicates
project status.

Closed offices — even cubicles — impede the line of sight among team members and to the project planning boards.

99

Open rooms are louder.
Discussions happen.

When the team is co-located, communication is quick and easy. No need to set up a meeting or play phone tag.

Make physical and temporal space for quiet work.

100

Think of "team" in broad terms.

Team members include:

Instructional Designers

Developers

Stakeholders

Agile Coach or Project Manager

Learners

Subject Matter Experts

Who else?

101

Move your SMEs in.

With Agile, you get very close to the project sponsor and/or SMEs in order to minimize meetings and wait time. It's not a bad idea to have them physically move in with you. That way they're around for daily standups, weekly meetings, and when you have a question and need a quick answer.

102

Reward effectiveness.
(not "perfection")

The project sponsor defines "perfection" and it's often not what we as trainers had in mind.